Quick Guides for Managers

Quick Guide #1

Write to Influence

Michel Theriault

WoodStone Press
Toronto, Canada

First Print Edition - ISBN 978-0-9813374-4-9

ebook version also available

Published 2012 by WoodStone Press

Summary Contents

The first part of this book focuses on techniques and approaches managers can use to improve their written communications to influence others.

This part introduces five specific things managers often write to influence others. For each one, there are specific ideas, samples and issues regarding what each of these five forms needs to be effective, drawing on the techniques in Part 1.

Table of Contents

Introduction

Managers need to influence others through their written communications on a daily basis.

The reality is that no matter how good you are at your job and how much you know about doing it well, those who communicate their management prowess through the written word and influence others will be more successful than those who don't—or can't.

Their organizations will also be more successful, a fact that bodes well for the organization as well as your managerial development and promotion.

In sum, to reach your full management potential, you must be able to communicate well via the written word and achieve results by influencing with those words.

This book is the first step.

Michel Theriault

Michel Theriault

Part 1 - Foundations

As a manager, you probably write every day. Whether it's a report, a memo or e-mails, the need to communicate via writing is a constant of the business world.

Many managers know their writing could be better. They communicate by writing because they have to influence someone—but they have little time to analyze whether their written communications does the job it needs to do. That's unfortunate. In reality, business managers do not need to be great writers. But they do need to be great communicators and influencers to have a positive impact on results.

Unfortunately, most of the contemporary manager's exposure to business writing in high school, college or university probably focused on the structure and mechanics of the writing process, not influence.

This focus on structure and mechanics versus message and influence effectively devalues the quality of a communications piece. As long the as the structure is sound and there isn't any spelling or grammatical errors, the piece works, right? Wrong. This approach misrepresents what communicating is meant to achieve. It treats the "effectiveness" of a communications piece as an extra instead of the main purpose.

In fairness, structure and mechanics are particularly important in business communications. Well-constructed communications that follow accepted guidelines for headings, spacing and numbering systems, for example, are graphic signals of the professional care taken to put a document together. Similarly, appropriate grammar and spelling also indicate that a document is to be taken seriously.

In sum, attention to structural and mechanical details demonstrates that a document was assembled with care because the writer wants its content to be taken seriously. That document, in other words, is *designed to influence* its readers. That gives a strategic function to your written communications because every single thing you communicate is truly meant to influence others.

Once structure and mechanics are mastered, this concept of writing to influence is an area most managers should target for improvement. Consider the number of times you've written an e-mail and received only part of the response you want. Let's say the receiver answered only some of the questions you posed or misunderstood certain points. Others may respond by peppering you with questions or denying your requests outright.

Too many non-influential managers deem "some action" a step in the right direction. Others might lick their proverbial wounds and then, incredulously, will forward back essentially the same e-mail (expecting different results). The strategic manager seeks influence and wants his communication to generate the compliance and understanding he needs to take a particular action.

This book helps managers develop a working strategy to improve their written communications.

Write to Influence

Don't just communicate, influence with your writing.

"The skill of writing is to create a context in which other people can think."
~ Edwin Schlossberg

Take what you think you know about communicating in your job and turn it on its head. You probably thought effective communication is all about being clear and concise so the recipient would understand your message. If so, you'd be wrong.

To be successful, you really need to think about your communications differently. You don't want people to merely understand what you write. You want to influence their action.

The business communications I learned in college focused on what I would call the fundamentals of structure. We learned how to format letters, the traditional headings to use in a business case and the general outline you should follow; purpose, findings, conclusion and recommendations, for example.

I also learned the right salutation to use for different situations, proper indentation, where to put the date, all about numbering for technical documents and how to write a nicely crafted (read: good-looking) paragraph and document.

That information is not a lot of help in the high-tech, fast-paced communications world of today, where e-mails and texts frequently replace formal documents.

Consider This

According to Wikipedia, *"Communication is the activity of conveying meaningful information."* In a business context, however, communication goes beyond conveying information and is meant to influence. In the workplace, mangers communicate to influence and get results.

Think about what you communicate in your job. Do you write procedures as an exercise in business communication— or because you want people to understand and follow your direction? If it's a particular action you seek, your real goal is influence.

Ditto for business cases, where you seek to influence a certain reader response, like approval.

The same goes for business letters, memos, reports and e-mails.

You want the correspondence to be readable, with good grammar and accurate spelling. But your primary goal is to get people to do certain things. You might seek their approval, want them to accept your recommendation or want them to take specific action. Regardless, your goal is influence—and action. The bottom line is that business managers use written communications every day. But not all of the tools we employ appear to demand the same structural formality of days past. What has not changed is the fact that managers must write to influence—and that should be a primary goal of every written communication, regardless of whether it's a formal business case prepared for a board of directors or a person-to-person e-mail.

What is the best way to deal with this reality? The first step is to know what you want done. Once a manager a clear about his goal, he can craft his communication to convey information—and to influence action.

Consider This

"The only people in the world who can change things are those who can sell ideas"
- Lois Wyse, advertising executive

The idea that communications is about "selling ideas" is critical. Managers often sense when they "need" to communicate about a certain issue. Unfortunately, too many then communicate without really thinking about what result they want to achieve and how they should write to achieve those results.

These managers seem to think that if they tell others about a particular problem, they'll know what the manager wants done. That approach is inherently illogical. Let's say a poorly-designed piece of communications material notes a need for budget cuts. Without an attempt to influence specific action, that communication may illicit a host of erroneous responses.

One person may think the manager is "communicating" about staff layoffs. Another might want to increase sales. Who is right? Who knows!

Managers typically attain their positions of organizational authority by strategically positioning themselves and their skills as company assets. That said, many also sell themselves (and their organizations) short by devaluing the role of strategic communications.

This problem is not new. Very few books or training programs about communication focus on influence as the primary strategic objective of the communication. Like most high school and post-secondary classes, they concentrate on how to convey information effectively—but they come up short when they define "effectiveness" in terms of structural and mechanical prerequisites.

While it is important that business communicators get the point across (and I'll discuss modern techniques to do that), it's more important to know *what* you are communicating, *why* you communicate, the *result* you are anticipating and how best to *influence* the reader to achieve your objectives.

These are the modern-day fundamentals of effective business communications.

The bottom line is that every time you communicate, you are selling something and you have to approach it from that perspective. Regardless of whether you're writing, giving a formal presentation or simply having a discussion with someone, your communications goals hold true.

Take this book as an example. I'm not merely using the book to convey information. I am trying to influence you to adopt a different approach to your own communication so you will be more successful in your career.

Write to get Results

Poor writing compromises comprehension and influence. It makes memos and letters easy to misunderstand or dismiss. Poorly-written e-mails are ignored. Overly-complex procedures fail to garner compliance. Postings and notices that miss the point are ignored. Business cases fail to convince and newsletters aren't read because they are deemed to be uninteresting. In every case, the "communicator" has failed to get the message across.

If you are not getting the results you need from your written communication, take a look at what you're doing. Assess whether you're using modern techniques to communicate and influence—or following what you learned in high school English classes or business communications courses that focused on structure and mechanics.

Accept that many of the traditional ways of writing simply don't work when you are trying to influence someone in the modern technological age. Moreover, way too many managers, sometimes compelled by the organization, launch a message before they identify the message's purpose. This is backwards. Excellent communicators assess the audience first, and then develop a message that will focus on the critical issue that audience needs to know and what will influence them to act.

Understand the Roadblocks

You are fighting against powerful forces that make it difficult to get your message across. Here is what you're up against:

Short Attention Spans

Get the point across quickly or you lose your audience's interest, since you are competing with others for their attention. This is also why you need to make it compelling, so they will become interested and give you more attention.

Information Overload

Since you are competing for their attention, your message must be uncluttered and simple to see, read and understand because everyone these days is bombarded with huge quantities of information. That's why your writing has to be well designed to convey your information efficiently.

Very Little Time

Nobody has time to read everything that crosses their desk. Long, tedious writing and presentations that don't immediately attract your audience's interest are a quick way to lose audience attention. If they think they have to invest too much time, they will put it aside, skim over it or not even read it, possibly simply going to the end to see your conclusion, losing your opportunity to actually influence.

Consider This

To earn success, be realistic about what you need to do to persuade your audience. Focus on content that hits the mark with structure that makes it easy to see and understand. If you're not sure your message works, test it with a trusted colleague.

When all is said and done, there are only three reasons a manager needs to communicate. You communicate to:

- ✓ Get approval or buy-in.
- ✓ Have your instructions followed, your request obeyed or action taken.
- ✓ Build a positive reputation.

If you can make these three things happen with your writing, you will be more successful. Use any of these three reasons to communicate as the basis for your approach whenever you write. They form the core of your strategy when developing communication tools.

Instead of worrying about spelling, fussing over grammar, trying to sound smart or following the same formats you see everyone else using, focus on what works for your audience.

Always emphasize content that hits the mark with structure that makes it easy to see and understand. Then, after you've done that, deal with the spelling and grammar, or get someone else you trust to polish it up. (Even the best writers have an editor.)

Think Strategically

The key is to have a strategy before you start. Writing without a strategy is like throwing darts blindfolded, just less likely to hurt your audience. You can improve your writing by following these key points:

- ✓ Be clear about your goal or message before you start to write.
- ✓ Provide information that is appropriate to the audience.
- ✓ Organize your information so it is easy to absorb.
- ✓ Be short and concise. Don't make it longer than it needs to be and don't use long sentences or big words.
- ✓ Consider what the audience wants to hear about, not just what you want to say.
- ✓ Don't assume too much. Spell out necessary details if there is any doubt or room for confusion.

Avoiding some of the most common mistakes is also important if you want to gain influence and recognition through effective writing. Here are the 7 Deadly Sins of Writing.:

1. Writing without a plan.
2. Writing what you want to say, not what the reader wants to read (and needs to know).
3. Trying to sound smart.
4. Writing too much fluff.
5. Choosing a structure that is difficult to read.
6. Making your key message hard to find.
7. Leaving the good stuff for the end.

Keeping these in mind, I'll outline some of the most basic—yet important—steps you must employ to influence with your writing.

Establish Your Purpose

Your message and goal must be integrated and guide your content and structure. Know what you want from the reader and make it clear. (e.g., I want you to understand x and do y.) For example, newsletters should be used to gain support for changes or show others how proactive you are. Your business case should sell your position to someone who can approve it. Your policy or memos must relay information in a way that ensures support and that your instructions will be followed.

Develop an Outline

An outline provides a kind of checklist to ensure you get all the information you need into your writing. It also helps you make sure the communication follows a logical flow and supports the persuasive (designed to influence!) nature of your writing.

The outline should be based on and supportive of the purpose you developed.

The outline ensures you provide the strategic elements you need to get your message across and influence your reader.

Those who write without an outline risk ending up with random, non-cohesive text. You may repeat things unnecessarily or not repeat things you should repeat. You may even forget to include some important information.

In sum, an outline is a strategic writing tool because it helps identify information you have to collect and include in your document. It also helps you write effectively and efficiently.

To create an outline, start with headings and subheadings that will become places to add content. The more details you have in your outline, the better.

Assess and Target the Reader

Understanding and assessing the audience is critical. You can't influence someone unless you know what will influence them.

Even the best ideas fail unless you communicate with your audience in a way they understand. This is not an easy task, but by looking closely at what the audience wants or needs to hear, you can tailor your communications for maximum effectiveness.

Consider how each element of your communication is received by the audience. This includes the level of detail, type of information, tone, wording and even the message. Keep in mind that your communications may span across different audiences with different needs.

Part of the planning includes understanding the audience's interest. For an article in a newsletter, the audience needs to know what the information conveyed means to them. The reader of a business case will want to know what decision is necessary and what impact it will have.

If a new policy is being communicated, the audience needs to know why it is being implemented, exactly what is expected, and what the processes for implementation will be.

Similarly, the content must support your purpose. Build your content with facts and examples that are meaningful to the audience and support the purpose for your communications.

Where possible, consider potential objections and build those into your communications up front. Don't leave unanswered questions.

Speak the audience's language and address readers directly. Focus on issues and information that will matter to them, not what you like and are comfortable with. Use examples they can relate to and avoid jargon they won't understand.

If you expect the audience or reader to take action, clearly outline what you expect from them and make it easy for them to take that action.

Prioritize Information

It's easy to pack lots of information into your communications, especially when you know the topic and are passionate about it. In the interest of keeping it simple and short, prioritize the information based on its potential influence and impact on the audience. Don't be afraid to throw out content that doesn't support your purpose.

Be sure the information you use is important to the audience. You want them to be motivated by what they read.

Techniques that Influence

There are a number of other very specific techniques you can use in your writing to improve your influence, many of which are based on social and psychological behaviors and have been proven by various scientific studies.

Whether you can use these will depend on the circumstances, but they are worth considering whenever you write something that needs to influence the reader.

The following provides some of those key techniques.

Hitting the Hot Buttons

Hot buttons are the most pressing and important issues facing the reader. They may not be the key reason you will influence the reader. But with a business case approval, for instance, hitting the hot buttons in addition to your message gives you a better chance of influencing the decision maker.

Hot buttons are different from the message. Hot buttons are based on the reader's issues, which may not always be the same as your message, but are also important for influence.

They must have a high impact with the reader, approval authority or stakeholders and while they may not be enough to influence directly, they should support your purpose.

When hot buttons are not obvious, take the time to engage stakeholders and staff to learn more about the underlying issues. Use the information you collect to develop your writing and shed fresh light on hot button topics.

Once you've identified the hot buttons and how you plan to address them within your writing so you can influence the reader, list them on a checklist to make sure each is addressed. When addressing hot button topics, take care to make sure they are not buried by other material or hidden in long paragraphs.

As noted in the section about how to best use format and structure, always use a heading, breakout box or other technique to direct the reader's attention to hot button topics and solutions.

Making Your Message Stick

You goal when writing is to ensure the reader sees, understands and most importantly, remembers the messages and arguments you want to influence them.

In the end, the best solution or initiative is worth little if you don't earn approval, agreement or compliance. As discussed earlier, you are competing for their attention with many other factors. You want the reader to easily absorb, remember and act on your message and arguments.

To make that more likely, there are techniques to make sure your message sticks. Several of these techniques apply to written communications as well. They are:

Keep it Simple

People remember simple things more easily than complicated, complex ideas and information. By keeping your language simple and using familiar terms, your message is easier to absorb.

When writing business cases, many management professionals use complex sentences, fancy language and long paragraphs because they believe their ideas need to sound formal and smart.

In reality, readers understand and absorb less information when you present it this way. These are often busy people with busy schedules and complex responsibilities. They do not have the time or energy it may take to read and re-read complicated documents—especially when these documents present solutions to *your* problems, not theirs. Simple and clear messages always have more impact and influence.

Keep it Real

It's tempting to use fancy language that's rich in concepts, promises and theoretical ideas. But your writing must be convincing. Even the busiest executive knows when something sounds too good to be true and if you lose credibility on one point, you risk losing it on your whole message.

For instance, for a business case, real examples and situations are the best way to get the attention of the approval authority. Procedures with real examples in the instructions help the reader follow the instructions. Concrete details and information in your memos, e-mails and letters will help influence the readers. Skip generalities and provide examples, facts and figures to make it more meaningful.

Keep it Honest

No matter how much or how little the reader understands about the issue you are writing about, they are likely to spot language that is less than honest or is wishy-washy. They are apt to be more aware of the underlying issues than many managers think. A weak business case won't stand up to the most cursory study and when it crumbles, it will take your reputation along with it!

Stick to the basics. Don't make promises you can't keep or statements that aren't backed by facts and evidence. If there are uncertainties, be upfront about them and outline how you manage or incorporate those uncertainties. It's better than having the reader think you are trying to slip something by them.

Strategic managers use communications, including written ones, to build credibility. To showcase your skills and managerial leadership, make sure the reader sees that you know what you're talking about. This makes it easier for the approval authority to believe and support what you say.

Make it Relevant

What you say will have a greater impact and is more likely to be remembered if you back it up with relevant examples and stories that are directly linked to what you say.

Rather than describing something, such as benefits, in general terms, find an example you can talk about. When you combine your statement with an experience, you build credibility and provide a relevant experience readers can relate to, particularly when making a decision or deciding whether to act.

Where possible, share a story about the issue you are writing about. Use illustrations, diagrams, flowcharts and graphs to clearly illustrate your points. These should support what you write and not just be added for filler. Keep them simple and directly relevant to the reader. Before including diagrams and illustrations, always have them reviewed by someone else. You want them to convey the message you intend.

Mirroring

This is a very important technique to use when trying to influence an outcome. Mirroring, which is intentionally adopting characteristics of the audience, helps the reader see, retain and use information they read in your communications. This recall will impact their final decision.

We see this technique in one-on-one selling, where the sales person will adopt some of the same positions as the person they are selling to. You can use the same concept in your writing.

Mirroring uses key phrases, terminology, issues and facts that are readily identifiable and already used by the reader. This approach helps them focus on the information you're providing by using the same terminology they know and understand.

If the reader isn't experienced in the managerial issues or topic you are writing about, shift to more generally-accepted terminology. When writing to influence, it is especially important to stick to terminology the reader is more likely to relate to and understand.

Consider This

Every industry has its jargon. When presenting a business case, for instance, avoid acronyms or terminology specific to your particular area of focus — unless you are absolutely sure the reader will understand. If you want to computerize a system, for example, zero in on what the change will mean. Tracking energy units, for instance, may be meaningless to an individual who thinks in terms of cutting costs and earning tax credits for energy conservation initiatives.

As part of the mirroring process, take information and terminology from your discussions with the reader and other sources if relevant. For instance, read your organization's mission, vision and values (MVV) statements, policy documents and annual reports to identify terminology and hot buttons and messages you can use to strengthen your business case.

Negate Concerns

The biggest mistake you can make is pretending negative issues or concerns the reader may have don't exist.

No matter how much you think your solution is the right one and you have all the issues covered, you can assume there are people who don't agree. Unfortunately, some of these people may be the ones you want to influence.

You must always consider what these concerns could be and take care to alleviate them with facts, figures and solid examples. When presenting in person, you can defend statements and positions when objections are raised. In a written document, the only real opportunity to deal with negative issues is when you're writing.

Consider This

The law of candor is the 15th law of marketing in *The 22 Immutable Laws of Marketing* by Al Ries and Jack Trout. The authors explain that an effective way of getting a positive reaction is to admit a negative attribute and turn it into a positive.

By identifying these concerns, and dealing with them up front and center, the strategic manager ensures that the reader's perceptions will be managed, not ignored. This is the best way to get your message across and it directly circumvents problems associated with negative assumptions that prevent your audience from being influenced by your writing.

Some of the negative issues you identify will come from the strategic analysis you do before you start writing.

When your analysis reveals an issue, always assume the perception will be negative—and then find a way to turn that negative into a positive.

Consider This

In "*Yes!: 50 Scientifically Proven Ways to Be Persuasive,*" the authors outline a number of high-profile examples, including a study by Kip Williams, a social psychologist. Williams's study revealed that juries were more likely to favor the defendant if their lawyers raised minor weaknesses in the case before the prosecution did.

Strategic managers may come across a negative issue, including one that appears to present a disadvantage, and be able to explain why it isn't negative at all. Even when you don't fully convince the reader, the willingness to raise and acknowledge a negative issue offers several advantages. Regardless of whether the reader is already aware of a potential issue, your willingness to bring it up makes you appear more trustworthy—and professional.

The Middle Choice

When you buy your coffee, soft drink, popcorn at the theatre or almost anything, you'll be offered choices that are designed to lead you to the middle choice. There will be a small, medium and large, budget, value and premium or similar types of choices. Retailers employ this well-established approach to provide you with choices that are designed to drive you towards the middle option, usually seen by buyers as the safest choice in their decision making process.

You can use this practice in your writing as well. When proposing something, you can propose a less acceptable solution as well as your preferred solution, with the intent of improving the attractiveness of your preferred solution. If the reader sees something that they don't like as an alternative, they will be more likely to say yes to your preferred option.

Give and Get Back

The principle of reciprocity is a commonly used technique whether you realize it or not. Bringing a colleague a coffee and then asking them to do something for you is a simple example. Doing something nice for your spouse before asking them to let you do or buy something is another example.

In a study by Dennis Regan in 1971, published in "Effects of a favor and liking on compliance" in the *Journal of Experimental Social Psychology*, Regan demonstrated this principle using a soft drink. The recipient of a free soft drink was more likely to buy a raffle ticket from the person who brought them the drink.

While you may be able to do this in writing, it's more likely that your written communication will simply refer to something you've already done for the reader before it asks them to do something for you. With some planning, you can use this technique effectively. And it doesn't only apply to individuals. When you introduce a new policy to employees, for instance, you can aid its positive reception by also talking about other policies or initiatives that benefitted them first.

Refer to Them Directly

The use of the word "you" is another very powerful sales tool managers should use when writing.

Most writers refer to clients using their company name, for instance. Some managers may incorrectly believe they don't even need to refer to the client at all. (They may rely on a kind of "form letter" approach to communications—and never even know how much less influential they are because of that decision.) The strategic manager understands that when it's time to make a point or demonstrate the value or benefits of his services, the word "you" goes a very long way to making your communications personal by speaking directly to the client.

For instance, instead of saying, "We will provide you with…" you should say "You will receive . . ."

Simply flipping around the reference and directly focusing on the reader gives your written communications more impact and influence. It also makes it easier for the reader to personalize your message.

Turn Facts into Messages

Providing facts or nuggets of information is a good way to provide evidence that influences the reader. But facts on their own don't contribute to the message you're trying to deliver.

Instead, explicitly relate the fact directly to the issue or message. Turn the fact into a benefit or use it to illustrate a risk and then take the time to describe exactly why this is a benefit or risk. If the facts are somewhat obscure or hard to relate to, give it some context by providing an example.

Quick Summary

Key Points ➨ Write to get approval, buy-in, have
instructions followed or to build a positive
reputation.

Executive   ➨ Start with a purpose and a plan to influence
Tips   with your words.

➨ Have strong content that gets your message
across.

➨ Make it easy to see your key messages.

➨ Use techniques that Influence

Traps to   ➨ Don't start writing until you have your plan
Avoid   and outline developed.

➨ Don't just focus on communicating, change
your focus to influence.

Your Action Plan

Based on what you've read, what do you plan to do to improve your ability to influence with your writing?

What are you going to do?	When

Notes

_____

_____

_____

_____

_____

_____

_____

_____

_____

_____

_____

_____

_____

Looks Matter

Nothing will influence your reader if
they don't see your message.

"Easy reading is damn hard writing." ~
Nathaniel Hawthorne

Strategy and great content are not enough to influence the
audience if they don't bother to read it. Because of the
audience's limited time, short attention span and information
overload, your job is to structure the information to be
compelling and easy to read.

In addition to compelling text, the strategic manager uses
structure to highlight their written material.

The format and structure of a communications piece plays a
key role in informing and then influencing the reader. Unless
the reader is able to clearly "get the point" of what you are
saying, your writing will be ineffective.

Why are Format & Structure so Important?

All business communication is meant to convince the reader
of something.

Structure is the visual representation of the information and
includes headings, placement of graphics and positioning of

key information. It also includes how you organize your writing, including the type of information you provide and in what order.

Format is the size and font of your text, margins, headings and subheadings. It's the indenting, bullets and other visual clues you use to give the text a professional look while drawing visual attention to certain information.

Structure and format make the information easier to read by doing the following:

- ✓ Help retention
- ✓ Lead the reader to your message
- ✓ Focus attention on what you want to influence.

Developing Structure

This includes lots of white space and enhances concepts and relationships with visual cues like headings, tables, diagrams and bullet lists.

Start with an attention-grabbing heading and then hit them with a powerful first sentence or paragraph. Don't save the best content for the last paragraph, or they may never read it. The idea is to convince them that they should keep reading. How you do this is part of understanding your audience.

Keep sentences, paragraphs and sections as brief as possible by only giving readers the information they need. Where appropriate, refer readers to other sources, such as a web site or another document.

Make your written material visually easy to read with short paragraphs, white space and simple language.

These structural and visual cues guide your readers to the message on which you want to focus their attention. When possible, use sidebars, boxes and pull-out quotes to highlight information and give the audience another quick hit of important information.

When writing reports, business cases or other long documents, use headings that are more descriptive than standard headings. For instance, use "Your Current Situation" instead of "Background," "Problems Being Solved" instead of "Objectives" and "Your Approval is Needed" instead of "Conclusion."

In longer documents, introductions and summaries will also help readers know where they are and where they are going. Don't be afraid to repeat important content or messages.

Overall Structure

The overall structure of your document should be planned with each section in mind. This basic information structure can be repeated throughout your document. This includes the following elements:

- ✓ Lead-in
- ✓ Detail / facts / arguments
- ✓ Summary or conclusion.

Consider This

Mirror excellence. When you come across documents, newsletters, trade articles or posted information you really like, study and learn from them. What catches your eye? What sticks in your imagination? What makes you care? How did the writer draw your attention to certain information? Imitation is the sincerest form of flattery.

Techniques

The ability to visually separate out information while making a document easier to read and the information easier to identify and absorb is a key purpose of structure.

Here are several techniques you should use to achieve those goals:

Chunking

This involves clearly separating sections, types of information or key information from your main text and visibly separating it.

You can do it using many different methods as described below. You can use headings, a text box, an indented paragraph, a separate graphic or a table. By using these techniques and highlighting them as necessary, either by separating from the main text or shading, bolding, etc., you will not only make it easier for the reader to absorb the information (i.e. in 'chunks'), you will be able to draw further attention to key information. This is an excellent way to visually highlight information.

Bookends

Bookends are short statements at the beginning and end of your document or sections. They help get your primary message across quickly.

Bookends can be used as an introduction and conclusion, or be presented as a brief message that appears before the introduction and after the conclusion. To make bookends stand out, put them in a box or use other formatting techniques (such as italics or a larger font) to separate the text and make it highly visible.

Bookends typically sum up the key point or main message of a section or document. You should use different wording for each end of the bookends—but do make the same point. This reinforces your message through repetition. It also provides a short, simple and obvious message that the reader is more likely to read and retain.

The best way to use bookends is to ensure they are visually different from the main text. You can use different font size, italics or shaded boxes like the example in this section. Your approach will depend on the type and formality of the document you are preparing.

In sum, bookends:

- ✓ Frame your point.
- ✓ Are the first and last paragraphs or statements, therefore are most likely to read and be remembered.
- ✓ Repeat your key message and arguments.

Bookends help get your message across, reinforce it and ensure it's easy to see and likely to be read.

Signposts

Signposts are another visual reference. They point the reader to information you want them to see and provide a reference point for transitions. The most obvious examples of signposts are headings and subheadings, but they do include other techniques identified below. All signposts break up the text and provide visual cues about the importance of a section or information.

Visual Structure & White Space

By leaving enough white space and creating a pleasing visual structure to your written material, the text will be easier to read and absorb.

You can increase margins, put more space between sections or paragraphs, or use columns or tables which open up your text. If you find yourself cramming information onto a page and making it dense and hard to read, re-evaluate whether all the information is actually necessary or extend it over a longer document, splitting it up into logical sections.

Headings

Make your headings meaningful where possible. Try not to use the same, boring headings in your documents. These are important not only to attract attention and get people to want to read what follows, but it also prepares the reader for what they will be reading, further improving retention of your message and argument, which helps you to influence them.

Dull, Boring Headings	Relevant and Meaningful Headings
Purpose	Why This Policy will Keep you Safe
Benefits	How You Can Benefit
Responsibilities	Your Participation will Keep Others Safe

Pull Quotes / Info Boxes

A form of chunking described earlier, this techniques highlights information that's important or enables you to add details you don't want to clutter up your main text with.

> **Get Attention**
>
> By using a text box, you can focus attention on a key point or include information that doesn't fit well in the main text.

Word processing software makes it easy to add these visual elements to your documents in many different formats and styles. You can position them anywhere within your text.

The "*Consider This*" boxes in this book are another example.

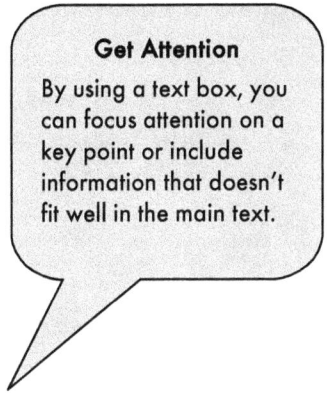

Bullets

Bullets force you to organize information and distill it down to the core of the message. It's also much easier for the reader to see your message since it isn't buried in a long paragraph.

Don't just use round bullets; other symbols that are built into most fonts, or part of special symbol fonts, can help convey your meaning, too.

➡ Bullets get attention.
   ✓ Bullets communicate your idea quickly.
   ☒ Bullets are easy to follow.

You can even use special graphics (icons or symbols) that are easy to add with your word processor but if you do, ensure the symbols are relevant and professional.

Tables (or table structure)

Some information is easily presented in a table format, which makes it clearer and more logical than writing several paragraphs. You can even nest tables within each other for more complex items.

Issue	Problem	Solution
Describe Issue #1 here	State the problem here	State the solution here
Describe Issue #2 here	Repeat as necessary	Repeat as necessary

Bold text

You can sometimes highlight specific words, phrases or terms within your text to provide emphasis and make that point stick out. **Use with caution**, however, since it can also be distracting and if used to often, this technique loses its value.

Charts/diagrams/figures

Charts and diagrams are an excellent way to talk about numbers, processes or other ideas that can be represented this way. Always make the charts or diagrams simple and uncluttered. You want to provide an easy visual reference and to focus on your message. Again, your goal is influence, not confusion!

Churn Rate %

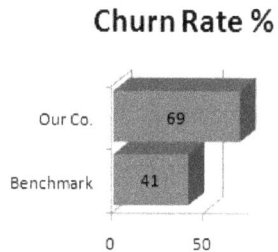

Boxing

Boxing involves separating information using a table structure that enables you to organize the information so it is easy to see. A simple structure also makes the data easier to comprehend.

Tables are easy to use and can be presented in line with the text as shown below, or floated with a wraparound feature similar to the text box used in the chunking example above.

This is especially effective way to present policies, procedures and other instructional writing.

This is a simple example of using the boxing technique:

Visual	It structures the information visually, separating it from the main narrative.
Easy to Find	Instead of being buried in the text, the information is easy to find.
Organized Structure	The technique allows you to easily organize information you might have otherwise included in a hard to read paragraph.

Step 1	Decide how to structure your information.
Step 2	Create a table with the columns and rows.
Step 3	Enter your information.
Step 4	Format the text and the table.

The Look and Feel

Lots of white space and visual cues such as the headings, tables, diagrams and bullet lists described above will enhance the look of your document while attracting interest in the concepts it presents.

This makes the document easier to read and makes it easier for readers to understand the relationships between the information presented.

Avoid long blocks of text, which are hard to read. Split them into shorter paragraphs or use subheadings. This highlights information and gives readers a quick visual clue about what's important.

These same techniques are often used in magazines and newspapers because they are a simple but powerful way to help readers identify important material within the main body of text.

Color

Where possible, use color to provide some visual cues and make your document more interesting to look at. But don't overdo it, as it can become a distraction. Also remember that your document may have to be photocopied or printed in black and white.

Margins

Resist the temptation to use thin margins to get more information into a shorter document. Thinner margins make a document more difficult to read—and can even impact others' ability to copy the material for wider distribution.

Wider margins increase white space. That option, especially when used with other formatting and structural techniques, will be more effective in the long run, even if it means you must add additional pages.

In some cases, a very wide left margin will even give you space to include small graphs, quotes and other information that are key to your argument. This effectively provides a two-column document, with the left-hand margin providing space for graphic detail (and adding white space!).

Font

While the differences seem marginal, serif fonts, like the one used in the main body text in this book, are supposed to be easier on the eyes according to research. They are commonly used in longer documents. San-serif fonts, like the headings in this book, are better for shorter documents or as used here, for headings and titles.

Using a different font for headings helps differentiate them better, along with font size. To avoid visual clutter, try not to use more than two fonts in a document.

You should also avoid fonts that are narrow or compressed. Again, these are more difficult to read.

Adding a little extra space between lines is another way to increase readability. This book has line spacing set at 1.1 times the normal. The line spacing is also formatted to provide an additional space between the paragraphs.

Readability

As you are writing to influence, it is essential for the reader to pay attention to and absorb what you're writing. Improved readability enables your reader to be more focused on what you want him or her to see.

The techniques above will all improve the readability of your writing, but it also plays an important role in forcing you to structure your thoughts, organize your information and develop a logical and clear flow to the document and your message. While your message and arguments need to have merit to influence the reader, better format and structure will improve the likelihood you will achieve your goals.

Quick Summary

Key Points
➡ Structure and format supports and highlights your efforts to influence.

Executive Tips
➡ Balance how your documents look and feel to achieve acceptance while also influencing the reader.
➡ Assume your readers have very little time or attention to read long, complex documents.
➡ Use your word processor's capabilities to its fullest to improve readability.

Traps to Avoid
➡ Don't simply use existing document formats. Update them with modern techniques.
➡ Don't try to entertain or sound smart, your job is to communicate and influence

Your Action Plan

Based on what you've read, what do you plan to do to improve your ability to influence with your writing?

What are you going to do?	When

Notes

_____

_____

_____

_____

_____

_____

_____

_____

_____

_____

_____

_____

The Mechanics of Writing

To Influence others, you first need to convey your message.

Proper words in proper places make the true definition of a style. ~ Jonathan Swift

While the content and structure of your writing are critical to successfully influencing with your writing, you still need to get words on paper.

This is often a source of frustration or anxiety, particularly for managers and their staff with either little experience or little aptitude to write. It's often a result of others emphasizing the need for above average writing skills, which is not really the point of writing to influence, as we will discuss below.

Forget What You Learned in School

Some of the traditional approaches for writing that you learned in high school or post-secondary business writing courses won't fit the needs of persuasive business writing.

With business writing, your primary goal is to communicate your message and arguments clearly and effectively so you can influence the reader. This takes precedence over "sounding smart" or trying to demonstrate your understanding of the English language, grammar rules, sentence structure, or a conservative business format.

While elements of grammar are important to avoid confusion and misunderstanding, it's more important to communicate effectively than to worry about all the rules.

Writing that is grammatically correct and classically structured but is difficult to read and obscures or buries the most important parts of your efforts to influence is much less effective than simple, plain writing.

Everyone has an Editor

You should keep in mind that even the best writers have editors, so you don't need to craft excellent writing on the first draft. Anything you and your staff write that will be used to influence others should be edited by someone else.

You are likely to write about what you know and love. This doesn't always translate into good communication. Because as a subject expert you understand the topic or issue so well, you may assume the same level of expertise on behalf of the readers. This leads to subconscious choices to leave out certain information, include other information or to structure text in a way that isn't clear to others.

An independent editor will be able to see these problems and identify spelling or grammatical mistakes and correct them before your document is read by anyone.

Writing to Persuade, not Sedate

As mentioned, readers have limited time or attention to read your document and digest your message.

You want the readers to focus their attention on your main point and arguments so they can be influenced by it.

Writing that is short, snappy, to the point, easy-to-read and visually appealing will get the reader's attention. In contrast, writing that is long-winded and complex will strain the reader's attention and retention. Similarly, large blocks of text with no visual cues to direct readers to important information will confuse, not educate.

In addition, you need to write so that the material is interesting. That's why examples and stories are important, as is visual material such as flow charts, other graphics and even headings that provide real information (versus filling space). The goal is to get your message across and persuade the reader. That persuasion will only work if the message isn't hidden in long, difficult-to-read and boring language.

There are easy techniques you can use to make your material easier to read:

- ✓ Use simple, descriptive words.
- ✓ Start sentences with action.
- ✓ Keep sentences and paragraphs short.

Another way to persuade rather than sedate is to provide clear, concise summaries of the information while steering clear of wishy-washy terminology. Focus on action and put images that demonstrate what you can do into the minds of the reader.

Spelling & Grammar

This book doesn't focus on spelling and grammar. While they are important, they are actually the easiest things to get right when compared to developing persuasive writing.

Spelling

Proper spelling ensures the right information is communicated. Because spelling errors may be associated with a lack of professionalism or knowledge, errors also prevent readers from taking your message seriously.

In reality, most people can "read around" spelling errors and typos because they understand what's been written. At the same time, many people view poor spelling as an indication that the quality of the message is poor as well.

The best way to circumvent issues related to spelling is to not worry about spelling when you are writing. Focus on getting your thoughts down and making sure your message is being communicated and you are influencing the reader. Spelling can be checked after the first draft and again before a document is released. If you are not comfortable doing this on your own, have a trusted colleague to do it for you.

Grammar

Grammar is more complicated because grammatical errors can confuse the reader or even make your point or message impossible to understand.

Grammatical errors may also have the same impact as spelling errors in that a document with grammatical errors may be dismissed as unprofessional—or unintelligent. This could have dire consequences in terms of a document's ability to influence readers.

Again, writers can get around this problem by keeping their written materials simple and short. Bullet points, numbered lists and graphics are important tools that help make grammar less of an issue.

Like spelling, leave grammar for the editing process. Once you've mastered your message, review your material to make sure you're following the appropriate rules. Use a trusted colleague to review your material and make sure that what you are writing makes sense to the reader.

Encourage your editors or proofreaders to point out ideas they do not fully understand. Get them to help you "get it right" before your material reaches its audience

Getting it on Paper

Written business material should catch the interest of its intended audience, but it need not impress anyone with its literary prowess. Focus on trying to convey your argument and influence the reader, not keep them entertained.

Using long sentences and fancy grammar detracts from your message and makes it less likely your audience will read or understand your message.

Keep it Simple and Eliminate Extra Words

Most people write like they speak. This often includes the use of complicated phrases, long words and filler words. Its worse when the writer believes that fancy language conveys a sense of importance or intelligence.

A quality editing process should help you eliminate the phrases and words that complicate your document.

Some examples include:

Hard to absorb	Easy to absorb
In view of the fact that...	because
In the event that...	if
Involves the use of...	uses
Institute	begin / start
To this end, we want you to...	Please...
...so that you...	...so you...

Use Picture Language

Describing what you mean in descriptive, or picture language, lets your audience visualize and understand your meaning without confusion.

Readers appreciate writers who can use a single word or a reference instead of complicated phrase. They also like it when writers use diagrams to illustrate a point instead of—or in addition to—extra words.

This doesn't negate the power of description. The more descriptive the prose, the more interesting the text. Interesting text is easier to remember because it helps readers form mental pictures. When writing, use picture language to improve your communication. Remember:

- ✓ Non-technical language is easier to understand.
- ✓ Illustrating with picture language supports your message.

✓ Write from the reader's perspective and focus on what they need to know and understand versus what you want to tell them.
✓ Do include comparisons / examples the reader can imagine.

Here are some examples where picture language will have a better impact than technical language for general communications.

Technical Language	Picture Language
Participation Rate	Number of people who participate
17 tons	The weight of almost 8 cars.
$2.9 million	The equivalent of 3 years of profit.
37 FTEs	37 new employees.

Speak Their Language

Never assume your readers know all of the acronyms or jargon you commonly use in your field. Other employees, customers, suppliers or senior management may not be familiar with them. To eliminate the chance of error, spell out the acronym or explain a term the first time it's used.

For longer documents, a glossary may be helpful. You can also explain an acronym or term via a sidebar on the page. Keeping these explanations separate from the main text helps maintain textual flow.

Short Paragraphs, Short Sentences

When presented with information, the human mind benefits from "breaks" that help us absorb the information properly.

When writers ignore this fact, sentences and paragraphs are often longer than they should be. This undermines the written document's ability to influence. Remember, your goal is to make the communication of information easier.

Your documents should not test reader intelligence to determine whether they can understand longer, complex sentences. Breaking your writing into separate ideas or pieces of information will make it easier to read and absorb.

This is especially important today, since information overload affects the amount of time we have to sift through the data that bombards us.

When drafting and then editing written material, look for ways to shorten sentences and paragraphs without making the text too short and choppy. Simplified sentences use fewer words to convey the message and eliminate unnecessary language.

Use Active Sentences

Always write with action in mind to convey a more powerful, action-oriented impression of your message. Avoid passive language, which typically uses more words and is harder to read and understand. Active language is:

✓ Easier to read.
✓ Conveys a positive impression to the reader.
✓ Shows action and boosts confidence in what you say.

Here are some examples:

Passive Language	Active Language
We are looking forward to working with you and implementing the new policy.	We will implement the policy with you.
The customer was given...	He gave the customer...
Our service will enable...	Our service enables...
Information is going to be provided in the meeting.	You will receive information at the meeting.
The air was tested by the specialist.	The specialist tested the air.
Upon approval of the business case, it would be our intent to commence working towards improvement of services right away.	With your approval, work to improve services can start immediately.

Quick Summary

Key Points ➡ Develop your message first, worry about grammar and spelling second.

Executive Tips ➡ Focus on your readers and how they will receive your message.

➡ You don't have to be a great writer to influence with your writing.

➡ Everyone has an editor, so get support to polish grammar and spelling.

Traps to Avoid ➡ Don't try to sound smart by using long, complicated sentences

➡ Don't focus on spelling and grammar. Get someone else to proofread your writing.

Your Action Plan

Based on what you've read, what do you plan to do to improve your ability to influence with your writing?

What are you going to do?	When

Notes

_____

_____

_____

_____

_____

_____

_____

_____

_____

_____

_____

_____

The POWER System for Writing

You can't influence if you can't convey your information.

> *I'm not a very good writer, but I'm an excellent rewriter. ~James Michener*

The best way to write effectively is to use a systematic process. You need to incorporate the techniques discussed earlier, but don't let those ideas get in the way of the fact that you need to get words down on paper. Blank pages will not influence others.

The POWER system introduces a structured approach and discipline into how you write. It will help you produce more effective writing with less effort.

Use this simple process when writing almost anything, from short memos or notices to complicated business cases or procedures.

The POWER system

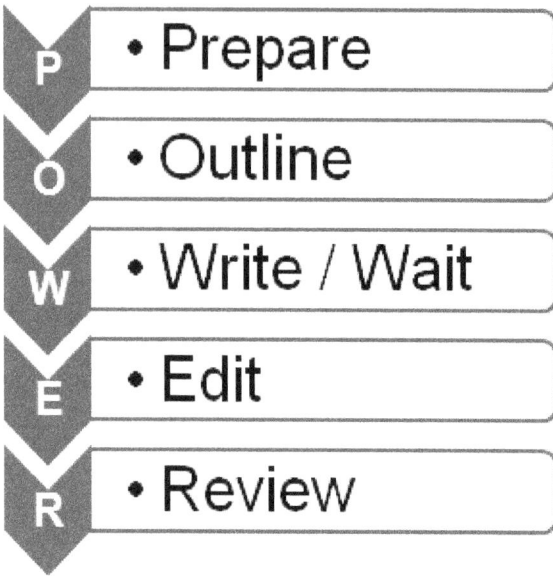

- **P** • Prepare
- **O** • Outline
- **W** • Write / Wait
- **E** • Edit
- **R** • Review

"Words are, of course, the most powerful drug used by mankind." ~ Rudyard Kipling

Prepare

1. Establish the purpose

2. Create your SOCO (Single Overriding Communication Objective) if relevant.

3. Analyze the audience.

4. Decide on messaging, themes, hot buttons, facts, evidence and arguments.

5. Collect your facts and supporting information, including images, samples, examples, etc.

6. Create compelling arguments.

Outline

1. Develop the overall structure and flow of your document.

2. Define the headings and subheadings that will cover all the information you need to include.

3. Identify the important information that needs to be highlighted.

4. Establish where tables, illustrations, bullet lists, etc., need to support your message.

Write/Wait

1. Use the outline to start filling in the information and writing the material.

2. Don't initially self-edit. First get all your information down on paper.

3. Periodically go back and compare your material with the original message and your outline.

4. Wait or move on to another section, leaving at least a full day before coming back to edit what you've written.

Edit

1. Read your original writing from top to bottom.

2. Do a rough edit on content, structure and format. Be brutal. Don't be afraid to delete material that doesn't matter. Copy deletions to another document if it makes you more comfortable —just in case.

3. Do a final edit and then check style and spelling.

4. Have someone else review your text and give you feedback.

5. Edit again.

Review

1. Reread your newly-edited material. Be critical.

2. Compare your text with your original purpose, SOCOs, themes and hot buttons.

3. Edit again if necessary.

Your Action Plan

Based on what you've read, what do you plan to do to improve your ability to influence with your writing?

What are you going to do?	When

Notes

_____

_____

_____

_____

_____

_____

_____

_____

_____

_____

_____

_____

Part 2 - Application

Knowledge, education and skills in your chosen field are critical to your success. But it's the soft skills that separate top managers from good managers because a top manager is able to achieve better results by influencing others.

As a manager, you write all the time, whether it's e-mails, letters and memos, procedures and policies or even business cases and justifications. The real purpose behind each written communication, regardless of its formality, is to influence others.

Using the writing, formatting and structural techniques described in Part 1 will help you contribute to your organization's success while simultaneously enhancing your career.

Whether it's you or your staff who do the actual writing, *you* and *your organization* will benefit from documents that are more effective and achieve the purpose you write them for, usually to influence others to agree, support, follow or approve something.

> *"Communicating without a strategy is like throwing darts blindfolded, just less likely to hurt your audience." ~ Michel Theriault*

.

Writing Memos, Letters and Postings

Never waste an opportunity to influence others.

> *"Bureaucrats write memoranda both because they appear to be busy when they are writing and because the memos, once written, immediately become proof that they were busy." ~ Charles Peters*

Memos, letters and postings are usually short and focused documents that address a specific issue. It could be a request, a policy or an opportunity to share important information you want the reader to follow or adhere to.

Today's business environment typically sees e-mail replacing formal letters and memos. Still, the formal letter or memo has its place and should be well crafted to get the results you want.

Postings are another important communications tool in many workplaces. Regardless of whether they're placed in elevator cabs, lunch rooms, health and safety notice boards, stores or other locations, postings often need to influence the reader, not just inform.

Give Them a Reason to Read

Always remember that you write e-mails, letters, memos and postings because you want people to read what you write. If these messages are specifically addressed to an individual, that shouldn't be a problem. An open letter, general memo or bulletin posting may be different. Here, you need to get their attention—but it's much more difficult.

One way to encourage people to read these documents is to always include a descriptive heading or title. In a letter, you may be tempted to use the common "re: what this is about" just before the salutation or first paragraph. That's technically correct. When writing to influence, however, this approach buries the descriptive heading such that it's not very visible.

If it's a general memo or posting, you might be tempted to add a heading such as "Memo," "Important Memo" or "Notice." But take note. Few people will be enticed to read it with those generic headings.

The heading should be highly descriptive and visible to draw the reader into your document so they want to read it.

Think about your heading as a newspaper headline and highlight the actual topic in the issue in a way that will attract your target reader's attention. Use that idea in big print at the top, such as "Parking Rule Changes."

Using a question is also very effective. Ask "Did you get your paycheck?" for a memo about switching from mailed checks to electronic deposits. Use "Can You Return It?" in a store posting to bring attention to return or exchange rules.

Short and Visual

To encourage your audience to read your materials, keep them short and to the point and make sure the first line or paragraph gives them a reason to keep on reading. Again, using newspapers as an example, this is your "lead."

Like the headline, the lead should be directly relevant to the reader and entice them to continue reading.

The rest of the letter or memo should be as short as possible and not look like a dense text. Use the techniques discussed in the previous section to make it visually interesting and readable.

Posted notices should avoid using typical letter or memo formats. Don't just take your memo and post it up on the bulletin board. Instead, make the posting big, bold and visual. This will help attract the attention of people walking by the notice on their way to get coffee or leave work at the end of the day.

Easy to Find Key Facts & Details

Make sure that important information is highly visible to the reader and not buried within the text itself.

Use bullet points, headings, graphics and tables as necessary to pull this information out and give it more impact. Even a one-page letter can benefit from this approach.

Eliminate Filler

Eliminate information that's not necessary to your point and your purpose.

Carefully consider what will matter to the reader and what will influence them. Make that information highly visible and then eliminate the rest.

Format for Clarity

The typical memo or letter format taught in English or business writing classes looks professional because that's what everybody's used to seeing. But don't let that format obscure your goal.

Key elements of your memo or letter include the date and title. They need to be obvious, but you can be flexible about their placement. Your primary goal is to communicate specific information.

Make sure the key facts and details of that information are highlighted and easy to read. Where appropriate, let graphic details like tables or charts carry your message and use large fonts to catch the reader's attention.

Letters, posters and memos that stand out from the crowd of other documents your audience receives will increase your readership—and influence. Dull documents and those that are difficult-to-read will hold you back!

Managers who regularly issue memos should design an effective format and then use it every time. This helps readers recognize your documents. They'll also know where to look to find key information.

Focus on the Reader's Needs

A common mistake managers make is including information they think is relevant or interesting, even though it's only of interest to themselves.

It's not easy to put yourself in his or her shoes, but when you write, always ask yourself whether the reader needs to know what you just wrote. Long documents aren't effective, so you need to keep out the useless stuff and only include things the reader will need in order to approve, agree or follow what you are telling them.

You may be passionate about what you're writing and want to include certain details, but often the reader won't be interested. Put your own interests and passion in check and focus on the reader.

Take the time to test what you write on someone who is closest to your audience. That can be someone on your staff, a colleague, or even one of your audience members. Getting their honest input will help you shape your message and succeed in your objective.

Answer Their Questions

Whenever you write for an audience, remember that individual members may have questions about what you are saying. Since you can't answer their questions while they are reading your material, you have to consider all the possible questions—and include answers in your material.

This will help satisfy their objections and enable them to agree, approve or follow your instructions without lingering doubts or questions.

Ask for Action

Memos and letters are typically written to elicit a response. Make sure your reader knows whether you're looking for approval, further information or even simple acceptance of your position. Effective memos and letters may put that expectation up front and then reiterate it at the end.

If formal approval is needed, provide space for a signature and ask them to send it back to you, for instance. If the due-date is critical, don't bury it in a sentence. Pull it out and make it clear and evident.

Example

This is an excerpt from a real letter about an issue with the office.

The first original letter is fairly typical of what many managers or their staff would write and reveals some typical errors in organization, structure and format.

The second revised letter is an improvement, using more white space, headings and bullets. The headings guide the reader from the problem to the obligation, risks and finally the deadline, or action required. The bullets make it easier to see the relevant details while the more open feel of the letter enables the reader to absorb it easily.

Original Letter

This is the original letter the manager used, based largely on the format and style that they found in the files when they took on the job.

Dear Mr. Wright:

We represent the Tenant on all lease related issues concerning the above noted location.

Our client reported that the temperature in the Leased Premises has risen to unacceptable levels (30 – 33 degrees Celsius) with the immediate probability of employees collapsing.

As per the Lease dated March 15, 1991, Schedule I, HVAC System:

> "1. The Landlord shall keep all parts of the Premises heated with artificial heat to a proper and reasonable temperature and provide air-conditioning, ventilation, and humidification in accordance with the following standards.
>
> Heating shall maintain an indoor temperature of 22 degrees Celsius +/- 1 degree Celsius temperature of 22 dry bulb......"

We are very concerned for the safety of our Tenant's staff and are therefore treating this situation as urgent and requesting that you take the necessary action in order to rectify this situation immediately.

Thank you for your immediate response in this matter.

Sincerely,

Revised Letter

This revised letter conveys the same information, but also focuses on key elements of the issue. The large heading is the first major change, then new headings were used to walk through the issue and highlight specific things, such as obligation, risks and deadlines.

Occupational Health & Safety Risk

Dear Mr. Wright:

We represent your Tenant at the above noted location and would like to bring your attention to an issue that needs resolution.

Temperature Problems

- The temperature in their premises has risen to unacceptable levels in the 30 – 33 degrees Celsius range, seriously affecting their employees.

Your Obligation

- The lease requires you to maintain a temperature of 22 degrees Celsius +/- 1 degree. Please refer to Schedule I, HVAC System for your obligations.

Potential Risks:

- This issue may escalate to an Occupational Health & Safety issue with Ministry of Labor involvement.
- This could become a breach of the terms of your lease with our Client.

Deadline:

- Please rectify the problem immediately.
- Advise us of your actions and how you will prevent this problem from recurring by August 3, 2007.

Thank you for your immediate response in this matter.

Sincerely,

This is an example of a very effective notice posted in a public area.

It covers all the key elements to draw attention, focus on the important information and answer the reader's questions. You'll see that the notice poses questions the readers may ask themselves. Using questions is a very effective way to draw attention to your information.

Service Changes
Late Nite

(F)

Aug 21 – 31
12:01 AM to 5 AM every night

No downtown trains at this station

How does this affect my trip?
- Trains run on the **V** from Roosevelt Av to 47-50 Sts.

- Take a Queens-bound **G** to Roosevelt Av and transfer to a Manhattan-bound **G** *or* walk to the 5 Av-53 St **E V** station where downtown **G** service is available.

Why is service being changed?
We are performing track replacement to ensure that subways continue to operate safely along the **G** line.

Quick Summary

Key Points   ➡ These documents are usually used to influence someone, so make them effective.

Executive Tips   ➡ Know your audience and write with them in mind.

➡ Have your purpose in mind and focus on what you want as you write.

Traps to Avoid   ➡ Don't use old and tired headings like 'Memo' or 'Important Notice.'

➡ Don't let your passion for the topic get in the way of writing something your audience will want to read.

➡ Don't bury the important information.

Your Action Plan

Based on what you've read, what do you plan to do to improve your ability to influence with your writing?

What are you going to do?	When

Notes

_____

_____

_____

_____

_____

_____

_____

_____

_____

_____

_____

_____

_____

Writing E-mails

A useful tool and necessary evil

"We communicate not by what we say, but by what the listener hears." ~ Waldo W. Braden

E-mail is one of the most pervasive and indispensable communication tools used in contemporary business. But e-mail is also surprisingly ineffective at communicating information or influencing readers.

The issue is not the tool itself. Providing almost instantaneous communication, e-mail can be one of your best assets if used effectively.

Make Subject Line Clear

The first thing e-mail writers must learn to do is to make the subject line clear to the reader. The sheer volume of e-mails received by most people demand a fast way to decide whether a specific message will be opened, saved, deleted or allowed to sink to the bottom of an inbox.

A highly compelling subject line makes an e-mail much more likely to get attention sooner. To optimize the subject line's value, use hot buttons and your understanding of the recipient's motivations.

Where appropriate, update the subject line to reflect new information or requests. When replying to an e-mail or forwarding it to someone else, do change the subject line to reflect the new recipient's interests when relevant.

Make sure the subject line is concise and include the keywords or phrases that will get the most attention. Where possible, include your call to action in the subject line.

Lead with Your Call to Action

Managers often leave the main point or the call to action (what you want the reader to do) to the very end of the e-mail. While you should have this at the end, you should also include it in the very first line of the e-mail. This ensures the reader knows what you expect of him or her.

Another way to make this clear is to include "Your Approval Required" as a heading. When that's not the case, you may want to write, "For Your Information–No Action Required."

Managers who are inundated with e-mails could get their staff to use this approach when sending e-mails to them. The pre-determined headings will help you focus on the e-mails that matter the most.

When action is required, don't be shy about making this clear at the end of the e-mail. If necessary, incorporate it in bold text.

Avoid Large Blocks of Text

People who understand the use of sentence and paragraph structure when writing letters sometimes forget this structure is also necessary in e-mails.

Long blocks of continuous text are very difficult to read, understand and retain. Instead, split e-mails into shorter paragraphs and sentences to make them easier to read. Use headings to break it into logical sections, topics or thoughts.

Keep it Short

E-mail should not be used for long communications. Where possible, keep e-mails short, to the point and focused on a single topic.

It may be more effective to send three e-mails, each with its own distinct heading, points and called actions, than to send a single e-mail which incorporates all three.

One of the reasons for including your call to action and germane point at the very top of the e-mail is that handheld devices, web-based and desktop e-mail software often have limited space to show the e-mail. Don't make the reader scroll down to find interesting stuff. Instead, put it up front is a way to entice them to scroll down and read additional information.

Use Formatting

Formatting is as important in e-mails as it is with other writing. Incorporating headings, bullet points, white space and even tables can make your e-mail messages much easier to read and understand.

Keep in mind that recipients of your e-mail may be reading it on a handheld device or tablet in a compressed size or in plain text format. Since some formatting may not come through on these devices properly, formatting should be kept simple.

For example, a bold heading may not show as bold. But if the heading itself was properly separated from the text, it will signal important information to the reader and help the reader navigate the e-mail. Colored text, images, tables and other fancy formatting won't show the way you intended possibly making it even harder to read.

You can test your formatting by sending yourself an e-mail and read it on your own device first. Then make any changes necessary to make it more readable in plain text.

Quick Summary

Key Points
➡ Your e-mail is more likely to be read if it is short and to the point.
➡ Your subject line should grab the reader's attention and make them want to read further.
➡ Tell the reader what you expect of them at the top (action, for information, approval, etc.)

Executive Tips
➡ Professional e-mails are just as important as professional letters.
➡ Include a call to action to drive the behavior you want.

Traps to Avoid
➡ Don't be long winded in your e-mails just because you can type well.
➡ Don't include multiple issues in a single e-mail or they won't all get the attention you expect.
➡ Don't use fancy formatting, since many mobile devices can't reproduce it properly.

Your Action Plan

Based on what you've read, what do you plan to do to improve your ability to influence with your writing?

What are you going to do?	When

Notes

Writing Business Cases

"The only people in the world who can change things are those who can sell ideas."
~ Lois Wyse, advertising executive

Business cases and other forms of justification used to gain approval for funding, resources and initiatives, can be an important part of the manager's responsibilities.

They are perhaps the most obvious in their importance, since successfully convincing senior management to proceed with your initiatives demonstrates your capabilities and your value to the organization.

While the success of a business case has much to do with the initiative itself, managers should also know that business cases are also judged on how the facts of that case are presented to influence decisions.

Here are some of the key principles you should use when writing a business case.

Use Relevant Headings

Most business cases follow a template. It may be a template used by others in the company, your predecessor, or be based on business writing models learned in college or university.

These templates usually provide standardized and generic headings for the various sections of the business case.

The manger who writes to influence does not waste the opportunity a heading provides. Instead, you should convert generic headings into more descriptive headings that become the starting point for how he influences readers to gain their approval.

Standard   Descriptive

Background	➔ *What's the Current Situation?*
Scope	➔ *Why is XXX a Problem?*
Objectives	➔ *What is the Expected Outcome?*
Options	➔ *What Solutions were Considered?*
Proposal	➔ *The Solution that will Work*
Benefits	➔ *Why this is the Right Solution*
Conclusion	➔ *Why Your Approval is Needed*

Know Your Audience

Part of the strategy involved with presenting a business case is to know and understand your audience so that your business case can be tailored to that audience for maximum impact.

For instance, if the CFO or other senior financial representatives in your organization must approve a business case, make sure it includes what they need to see. Draw their attention to information about cost analysis, revenues and pay back. Deal with topics like capital and initial or one-time costs.

In essence, anticipate their questions—and provide answers. You should also know the hurdles they want to conquer. Are they looking at a maximum number of years they expect for payback? Will they need to calculate inflation estimates?

If your audience is nonfinancial, approach the business case with an understanding about their stake in your business case. Make sure that you discuss anything that will matter to their specific set of responsibilities. If the vice-president operations is very concerned about risk, your business case should address this risk and describe how the risk is mitigated.

Also consider any hot buttons with the audience who will be approving your business case—and address these issues up front. If environmental stewardship is a key issue, your business case should address environmental stewardship.

Provide Convincing Details

Never forget that those assessing your business case are looking for facts and details. These are what make a business case compelling. If you have facts to support approval of your business case, make sure these facts are presented in a way that influences your audience to give approval.

Where appropriate, use visual aids to clearly present the facts in a way that effectively represents your business case. Instead of including numerical information in narrative form within a paragraph, break it out and provide it visually in a graphic.

This could be accomplished with a chart or table that's organized to highlight the positive aspects of the facts and details you're presenting.

Deal with Objections

You may get to formally present your business case and discuss it with the audience. When writing it, however, you must assume that you've opened a one-way conversation and that you will not have an opportunity to clarify or explain any elements of your business case that are confusing, uncertain or lack information.

The biggest mistake you can make is pretending issues or objections don't exist. They will negatively affect your ability to influence the reader.

Instead, think about the objections or issues that could arise with your business case and use your written business case to respond to them directly. While it's not always easy to identify potential issues, do try to consider as many potential objections or negative issues as you can.

Some of these will come out of your analysis of the issues and from discussions with the stakeholders as you develop your business case. Others may be harder to find. Talk to your colleagues and your staff and run your initiative by them.

Ask them to play the devil's advocate and try to punch holes in your business case. Use this input and deal with the issues raised by incorporating them into your business case.

Also remember to deal with these issues head on. Don't bury issues or objections within your narrative. Create a section or use headings that clearly indicate that you've identified and acknowledged potential problems and have valid responses to the issues.

Identifying potential concerns and dealing with them accomplishes two things. First, it moves your business case one step closer to approval. Second, it boosts awareness of your leadership skills and gives the approval authority more confidence in your abilities.

Leave Things Out that Don't Matter

As a manger, you are probably very passionate about the topic of your business case. While this passion is very valuable, it can have a negative effect on your written business case if you don't pay attention to what really matters to the audience.

Your passion may, for example, promote a tendency to include either too much information or too many details. This reflects your interest and detailed knowledge of the topic and the issues related to the business case.

Unfortunately, this kind of information overload may be irrelevant to the merits of the business case. Including too many details may water down the impact of the items that are most critical to the decision.

For instance, you may come up with nine points that support your business case. If the three points are what's really needed to support approval of the business case—and are the only points your audience cares about—the other six points may be distracting. Icing on the cake is nice. But do take care to make sure you're not overdoing it!

To avoid a loss of influence, carefully assess the other six points to determine whether or not they will make a difference in the decision. If you don't think they will, eliminate them or add them to a separate section or to the appendix as supporting material.

Call to Action

Since the purpose of your business case is to get approval, a well-written business case must make that request for approval very clear. You should also provide a means for supplying that approval.

Some organizations have a formalized approval process complete with formal signature blocks. If this is the case with your organization, add that signature block as a cover sheet or incorporate it within your business case. Never leave this step to someone else.

If there is no formal process, develop your own by providing a place for signatures at the end of your business case.

Include a call to action just ahead of the signature. This ensures the signatory knows you are formally asking for approval. Don't leave it to chance.

Quick Summary

Key Points

➡ Include only information and arguments that are likely to influence your audience. Leave everything else out.

➡ Consider what the objections might be and be sure to deal with them.

➡ Provide evidence and details to convince the reader and make it easy for them to see.

Executive Tips

➡ Talk to the decision makers in advance to find out what it will take to get your approval and build it into the business case.

➡ Ask for their approval; even provide a signature block if possible to get them to sign on the dotted line, even if it isn't binding.

Traps to Avoid

➡ Don't include information that isn't directly relevant or likely to influence.

➡ Don't write a long business case that isn't likely to be read in detail.

➡ Don't use old style headings; switch to headings that grabs the reader's attention.

Your Action Plan

Based on what you've read, what do you plan to do to improve your ability to influence with your writing?

What are you going to do?	When

Notes

_____

_____

_____

_____

_____

_____

_____

_____

_____

_____

_____

_____

Writing Articles or Newsletters

"Good communication is as stimulating as black coffee and just as hard to sleep after."
~ Anne Morrow Lindbergh

Management professionals communicate with a lot of people on a daily basis. Still, targeted communications to your employees, customers, suppliers, industry colleagues or others is often at the bottom of a long list of priorities.

While the newsletter (or articles) is an often-overlooked and highly-underestimated tool for communicating, strategic managers understand how it can be used to promote issues, enhance reputation and support other initiatives.

Newsletters that are well laid-out and well-written will inform readers and deliver your message. Articles can focus on telling the reader what you are doing for them (things they may take for granted) or reminding them about initiatives, services, policies and other important information.

While the underlying reason for using a newsletter may be different for different types of audiences, the fundamentals are the same: you need to get them to read it first, then you need to get your message across and achieve your purpose.

It's all About the Content

It often seems like the decision to start a newsletter is made without understanding how to use it as an advantage or without knowing what its key messages will be.

This results in a scramble for content and poorly-focused articles on items of little interest. This is a recipe for disaster as your audience won't read future newsletters they've already judged to be useless and uninteresting.

The strategic manager launches (or re-vamps) a newsletter with a purpose and a plan for success. By understanding the need for effective communications, you can determine the goals and actively seek articles that carry their messages forward.

Managers who want their newsletters to serve as a strategic communications tool should consider the following tips:

1. The newsletter is a sales opportunity. You should use it to gently promote your purpose.

2. Write the newsletter for the audience. Don't use jargon or technical language, which will confuse more than it educates and informs. Ask yourself "why should they care?" and write it with that question in mind. Your readers care about different things than you do.

3. Use catchy headlines. Look at newspapers, magazines and even other newsletters for examples of how to write headlines that attract attention. If the

title looks boring, people won't read an article's content.

4.   Use titles that are descriptive, like "How this affects you" or "What are your alternatives?"

5.   After enticing them with a catchy or thought-provoking title, make sure the first sentence or paragraph makes them want to read the rest. Don't assume they want to read it just because it's from management.

6.   Write tight and skip the fluff. Your job is to communicate efficiently, so don't worry about impressing your reader. Organize your information with headings and bullets instead of long paragraphs. Make sure the important information is easy to find.

Content Checklist

The most important part of a newsletter is content. Use this checklist as a guide to improve your content.

✓   Does your headline catch the readers' attention?
✓   Is the first sentence or paragraph of the article likely to entice the reader to continue reading?
✓   Does the article deliver your message?
✓   Is the article concise and to the point?
✓   Is your message repeated within the article and throughout the newsletter?
✓   Does your article speak directly to the reader and make the article personal instead of using general language?
✓   Do the photographs and graphics add to the article or are they filler?

✓ Does the article use active sentences instead of passive ones?
✓ Are you avoiding the technical terms and acronyms that readers won't understand?

Producing Your Newsletter

You can produce newsletters with high-end layout software such as Adobe InDesign, low-cost desktop publishing programs like MS Publisher or even word processing software. For small newsletters, MS Publisher is ideal, since it is easy to use and its many templates mean you can focus on content versus the creative part of the newsletter.

To decide on the size of your newsletter, take into account how much content you will have for each issue, and whether occupants will read more than a page or two. The format depends on how much content you have. For a one- or two-page newsletter, standard 8 ½" x 11" paper will do nicely. For a three- to four-page newsletter, consider an 11"x 17" sheet folded in two.

Keep your layout simple and professional, using "white space" to make it easy to read. A two- or three-column format provides flexibility and is also easy to read. Stick with standard fonts and use them consistently.

If you send the newsletter out in an e-mail, avoid attachments or links as people seldom click on them. If you must, then include the headlines and first paragraph as a teaser, then provide a link for them to follow to the article or newsletter on-line or to download the PDF version. If you have an e-mail with several long items, list the headings with the teaser paragraph and then include the full article further below.

The frequency of your newsletter is important. Don't plan a monthly newsletter if you can't fill it with useful content. When starting, avoid scheduling the newsletters; simply publish them when there is something to say, or for specific communication purposes.

If you distribute by e-mail, consider sending shorter items more often versus following a quarterly format. In this case, your subject line becomes your catchy heading.

Sample Newsletter

This sample was created with inexpensive layout software using a free template.

FacilityNews
ACME Dital Forms

this issue
Conference Room Booking
New Security Measures
Your Exercise Room Renovation
Are you Helping the Environment?

Annual BBQ

On June 2nd, join your Facilities department from 11am to 1pm on the patio at the south entrance for free hot dogs, hamburgers and pop. This is your chance to ask us about your upcoming move!

You are using Green Power!

You can feel good that whenever you use electricity at ACME, it's from green sources.
On your behalf, we now buy our electricity from a green power supplier who only uses solar and wind power.

Need a Room?

You may not know that we have a board-room booking system. It seems not many of you are using it, resulting in lots of problems when people need a conference room.

Don't get kicked out because you don't have a boardroom reservation.

Instead, book your room ahead of time online through the intranet. Don't know how? Call our Help Desk and we'd be happy to walk you through it.

Help Desk : x7883

Don't Get Locked Out

For your safety and security, we've been installing new security measures throughout the building. You will need to have your card to get in through the back entrance near the parking lot at all times and to access the building after hours and on weekends.

What's Happening?
New card readers are being installed to increase your safety and security
When it's happening?
Beginning July 1st
What do you need to Do?
Book your appointment to get the new access card and be sure to have it with you at all times

Want your Carpets Cleaned?
Our cleaning company is deep cleaning the carpets on May 3rd and 3rd. The only thing you need to do is move any boxes or other stored items from the floor so they can get the job done.

Tips for Writing your Newsletter

Write a Catchy Heading

Use headings that actually say something and make the reader want to read more.

This catches your attention	This one doesn't
Better Heating This Winter	Capital Projects

Write a Strong Lead Paragraph

Use a strong lead paragraph when writing about anything. The lead captures the readers' attention and gets them to read the rest of the article.

This makes you want to read	This doesn't make you read
This winter, your heating comfort will be vastly improved due to a project initiated by	The boiler project, which was started February 1st, was finally completed on March 4th, 2010 by John Q. Construction Inc. ...

Speak Directly to the Reader

Speak directly to the reader by avoiding general references.

This speaks to the reader	This doesn't
Your heating comfort will improve	Building comfort will improve

Don't use Terminology

Remember who your audience is. Use terminology they are likely to understand and explain quickly and briefly when necessary. Don't include information that doesn't matter to them, such as a contractor's name, etc.

This uses terminology	This doesn't use terminology
The coal fired low-pressure boilers were replaced with a high-efficiency gas boiler with a new GUI interface BAS system and remote access through dial-up remote from a handheld PDA.	The project includes a new boiler that supplies hot water to the radiators and a new system that separately controls each radiator to improve control over the temperature in each area.

Show Action

The text must show action. Use active language instead of passive language.

This shows action	This one doesn't
We are replacing the boilers.....	We will be initiating a project that will replace the boilers.....

Frame your Subject

Newsletters are meant to communicate and should get a message across. Repeat your message at least twice, depending on the length of the newsletter item. Within reason, use the old adage "tell them what you are going to tell them, tell them, then tell them what you told them."

The first Sentence	The last Sentence
This winter, your heating comfort will be vastly improved due to a project we've initiated.	With the new system, we are confident you will be more comfortable this winter.

Tell Readers why it Matters to Them

You need to figure out why they should care about what you say—and then tell them why. Focus your writing on the impact to readers and how it will improve things for them.

This example tells them why	This example doesn't
Your comfort will improve now that we can separately control each radiator to set your area to just the right temperature.	The Controls project will improve our ability to separately control the radiators and regulate the temperature independently.

Quick Summary

Key Points ➡ Boring newsletters won't be read.

      ➡ Create newsletters that interest your audience.

      ➡ Make them easy to access through multiple methods, including e-mails and PDF documents, for instance.

Executive Tips ➡ Use the newsletter to sell what you are doing for them.

      ➡ Speak directly to the audience, including issues, language and terms they understand

Traps to Avoid ➡ Keep it short; one or two pages are ideal.

      ➡ Don't set regular dates until you are sure you can keep up the pace.

Your Action Plan

Based on what you've read, what do you plan to do to improve your ability to influence with your writing?

What are you going to do?	When

Notes

_____

_____

_____

_____

_____

_____

_____

_____

_____

_____

_____

_____

Writing Procedures

Procedures are a strategic tool to manage services.

"We should work on our processes, not the outcome of our processes." ~ W. Edwards Deming

Procedures (and policies) can be an important part of your responsibility. They improve consistency, enable training and cross-training, make it easier for someone to fill in for an absence and provide a means of explaining / defending your approach to many controversial or unpopular policies.

They also provide concise instructions to your employees, colleagues or customers.

Unfortunately, if they are long and difficult to follow or understand, they won't drive the compliance and acceptance you want.

Keep them short and simple so they are useable. Many managers think more is better. Unfortunately, that approach is more about show than results.

For successful procedures, you need to write them with the same techniques you would use to influence others–after all, your goal is to influence them to follow your procedure.

Quick Guides for Managers **107**

If you haven't developed your procedures yet, take a simpler, shorter approach to developing them. If you already have a bookshelf full of procedures, operations manuals and other similar documents, leave them on the bookshelf and develop an overlay with the key parts of the processes noted in an easy-to-use, easy-to-reference format. Then use them for your training, performance and continuous improvement processes.

Managers who solicit user input are more likely to get buy-in. That approach also yields better procedures that are more likely to be understood and followed.

Get into Their Heads

Real-world experience beats theory every time. What you think should be included or outlined a certain way may not align with the needs of those who use your procedures. This is similar to the principle of influence where you consider the message from the reader's perspective.

To avoid future problems, get the people who will use the procedures involved in developing them in the first place, or test your procedures with them and change/modify based on what you learn.

If something is hard for them to understand, it's not their fault. It's because you haven't clearly outlined it.

It's hard for people to follow and comply with your procedures if they don't understand them. Getting this right is important.

Keep Procedures Short and Simple

As discussed earlier, short, concise documents are easier for the reader to absorb and understand than long, tedious ones.

There is no reason to "dumb down" policies and procedures but busy people should find the documents easy to use.

If you honestly believe that a higher level of detail is needed, then build your procedures in layers. Start with a simple version that gives the user an outline of the procedure in simple, compact terms. Using all the techniques you've learned, add additional more detailed layers or develop the documents in sections that make it easy for users to access and follow on their own.

Like other writing, the format of your procedures will significantly impact the reader's ability to follow what you're saying.

Simple flowcharts, tables, illustrations, meaningful headings and clean, well-structured documents will help meet this goal. Suggested checklist, flowchart and document formats are provided below. Try to get away from a simple text-based structure that's narrative-focused and paragraph-dominated.

Checklists

A checklist provides the simplest implementation of a process or procedure. Checklists can be a stand-alone guide or part of an overall process.

Checklists are a simple, visual tool to outline key steps required for any given procedure, or key items that need to be completed, filled in or otherwise considered. Checklists can help even the most experienced people successfully complete important steps. If possible, keep them on separate pages so they can be printed and used separately as a working tool.

Paragraphs, narrative and other formats simply aren't as effective, since they take more time to read and understand. When you use a checklist as an overlay to the overall procedure, it makes the procedure much easier to follow.

Involve your target audience and develop checklists based on items that really matter, not everything you can think of. Short checklists are better than long, tedious checklists. Where checklists would take multiple pages to complete, break the lists into sections on separate pages.

The best example of checklists is in the aviation industry where they are used to make sure even the most experienced pilot doesn't miss a detail that can result in catastrophe.

Some people with experience don't think they need to follow a checklist. Research shows that even experts make mistakes, so checklists have proven their value time and time again. In the book, *The Checklist Manifesto*, Atul Gawande provides compelling statistics with very clear examples of where a simple checklist gets results even for seasoned, well-trained medical specialists who supposedly know what to do in every situation.

Mr. Gawande discusses examples of how using a simple checklist in the operating room has reduced infections and medical errors by significant margins. It shows that even the most highly-trained and skilled professionals can benefit from a checklist.

The key is to use simple, short and easy-to-use checklists. In many cases, a checklist provides quick assurance that the key elements of the process have been completed.

You can create checklists on a word processer using checkmark or box bullets, using tables or even a spreadsheet.

They can be used in many aspects of management, including the following situations:

- ✓ To verify that all information has been collected for a process such as issuing a monthly parking pass.
- ✓ To verify that all the steps required are followed before something is done.
- ✓ As a quality-control inspection after a project or task has been completed.
- ✓ To verify all parts of a form have been filled in.
- ✓ As a double check that each step has been completed properly.
- ✓ As an audit tool to ensure compliance.

Here is a simple sample checklist maintenance staff in an office can follow after they have completed work:

- ☐ Did you clean up the work area?
- ☐ Did you put the customer's furniture back in place?
- ☐ Did you leave a comment card on their desk?
- ☐ Did you advise the client that the work is complete?
- ☐ Did you check the room to identify any other issues to correct?

Graphics & Diagrams

In addition to checklists, include simple flowcharts and diagrams to illustrate the process, steps and decision-making process. Flowcharts are easy to make with standard word processing, spreadsheet or presentation software, so use whichever you are most comfortable with. You don't need specialized software, although it can make graphics and diagrams easier to create and update.

The following sample process diagram is called a Swim Lane diagram or Cross Functional Flow Chart. It clearly identifies each individual's steps in the process, helping the reader to clearly see their specific responsibilities and the interactions. This can replace or complement a written narrative in some cases.

This particular flow chart was created using a spreadsheet program, but you can easily use other programs that enable graphics, such as some graphics programs, word processors and presentation software. If you do more than a couple, you should invest in a specialty program for creating flowcharts.

This example shows that while specialty software makes it easier to design a flow chart, it's not a requirement:

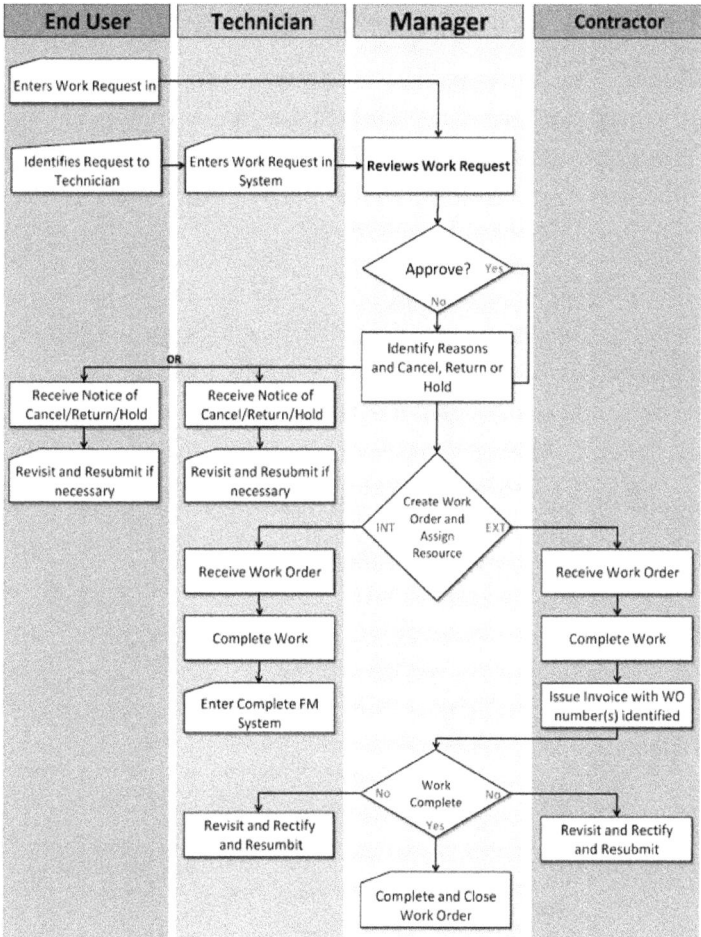

End User	Technician	Manager	Contractor

Enters Work Request in

Identifies Request to Technician → Enters Work Request in System → **Reviews Work Request**

Approve? Yes / No

Identify Reasons and Cancel, Return or Hold

Receive Notice of Cancel/Return/Hold / OR / Receive Notice of Cancel/Return/Hold

Revisit and Resubmit if necessary / Revisit and Resubmit if necessary

Create Work Order and Assign Resource — INT / EXT

Receive Work Order / Receive Work Order

Complete Work / Complete Work

Enter Complete FM System / Issue Invoice with WO number(s) identified

Work Complete — No / No / Yes

Revisit and Rectify and Resumbit / Revisit and Rectify and Resubmit

Complete and Close Work Order

When designing flow charts, make sure they are easy to read. This makes it easier for users to see what they should do or not do and that increases the effectiveness of your procedures.

Format & Structure

A table structure similar to the samples shown below makes it easier to read and understand work processes and directions. This approach forces you to think about the processes in a logical, structured way and that also improves your documentation.

The sample below shows the overall structure. Instead of headings on top of the text, the headings are to the left, making it easier to find what you are looking for. Other information is presented in the same way, but nested within the original table.

While the structure could result in a longer document, it will also be easier to read. If document length is a concern, challenge yourself to shorten your text to include only what's necessary.

PURPOSE

OBJECTIVES	Work Orders address maintenance or service requests which require the repair or replacement of building components, finishes or systems which have failed in order to bring it back to original standards, restore services or prevent service failure.
	Work orders include service requests which may not be related to building system or component failure however must be performed by suitable qualified staff and are required to enable ongoing activities at the schools.
OTHER REFERENCE DOCUMENTS	The following lists other documents you may need to reference related to this procedure:

Reference Document	Why you may need it
Purchasing Procedures and Manual	Provides direction on when a separate procurement initiative will be required to procure a contractor services for any given work order requirement.
Level of Approvals	Documents authority levels for approving contract work / invoice payments
VisionFM manual	Provides detailed information on the use of the work order management system.

Here is another example of using a table to present information. This clearly identifies the types of priorities and their related descriptions. Note that the wording is stripped down to the key information. There is no need for long paragraphs.

PRIORITIES

Priorities are assigned to each work request based on the following criteria:

Priority	Description / Guidelines
High	Will cause damage to persons, structure or equipment if not corrected
	Will have a negative impact on school activities if not corrected
Medium	May cause future damage to persons, structure or equipment if not corrected
	May have a future impact on school activities if not corrected
Low	Does not have an immediate impact however should be corrected to preserve asset life

The responsibilities of each individual in the overall process can be described using language that's similar to that used for the job description for the roles. Note the use of simple, shortened descriptions. Details for each of the specific steps or responsibilities can be outlined separately in the process. If needed, the list can be split into two columns with additional information for each responsibility added.

The table format in the next example makes it easy to structure information:

PRIMARY ROLES & RESPONSIBILITIES

MANAGER		
	1.	Reviews new Work Requests
	2.	Respond to all related requests and issues
	3.	Determines whether to use internal or external resources.
	4.	Distributes Work Orders to Internal; and External resources
	5.	Reviews work orders that have not yet been completed
	6.	Closes work orders following verification of work complete and correct invoicing as appropriate
	7.	Review completed work orders and if additional work is required, authorizes the work

The next example lists specific actions that each work order can go through. Again, it is simple, clean and easy to reference and gives a straightforward overview. If necessary, each of the actions could have its own heading further below with more details.

WORK REQUEST ACTIONS

There are a number of actions that can be taken with any given work request. These are described below:

Action	Description
Return	The work request is returned to the originator for more information or clarification. The originator can re-submit or cancel.
Hold	The work request is on hold pending additional information before processing.
Cancel	The work request is cancelled because it is a duplicate, the work is no longer required, the request does not fit the criteria of the work performed by Facilities Management.
Assigned	The work request is approved and the work order is assigned to a resource who will complete the work.
Complete	The work identified in the work order has been completed
Closed	The work has been completed to satisfaction and no further activity is required.

The following table is a text version of a work flow, along with a brief description. This could be accompanied by a

Swim Lane flow diagram, similar to the one shown further above.

Main Steps

Overall Workflow Steps

The following chart outlines the main steps involved in the complete cycle of a work order, along with who is involved and a general description of the step.

Each of these steps is further described in more detail in the next section, along with decision points, information requirements and handoff.

Step	Who is Involved	General Description
Generate Request	Custodian, User	This step generates a work request for work to be performed and is the initiation of the work order process.
Review Request	Manager	In this step, the work request is assessed against established criteria and a decision is made on how to handle the work request.
		This may include returning it for more information or clarification, denying the request or cancelling it.
Assign Work Order	Manager	If a work request is approved, the next step is to create a work order and assign it to a resource who will complete the work.
		Resources are either internal Facilities staff or external contractors as required. There may be more than one work order created from a single work request.
Complete work	Custodian	The resource who has been assigned the work order completes the work identified on the work order.
Verify completion	Custodian	Where the work is done by an external resource, the work is to be inspected or otherwise verified that the work is complete satisfactorily before closing the work order and paying the external resource.
Close Work Order	Manager	Once the work is complete and verified, as appropriate, the work order is closed to indicate that the work order is completed to satisfaction.

While the examples provided above are fairly simple, you can use the techniques of tables (with nested tables when necessary) for any of your policy or process requirements. For instance, you can make the manager's role description more extensive by including a table which has boxes/rows for different types of responsibilities.

User Involvement

Developing procedures doesn't have to be a long, complex process. As indicated earlier, start with the people currently involved in the process to write down the steps they take or to quickly draft a flow diagram to get you started. Ask them about the key steps and the decision making required during the process. Be sure to ask them what they would do differently if they could.

Compare the flowchart and steps from everyone involved in the process and then meet together to go over the steps to identify common ground. Make sure hand-over points and information requirements are clearly noted.

Then use the tools above to document the process as described. After it's done, walk through it with your team and make sure it reflects the correct procedures. Improve it where necessary.

Finally, make sure you make these documents easy to find and reference. Whether it's on your company's intranet site or in binders, key processes and steps should be easy to find and reference and not be buried in lengthy documents. Use separate files or tabs in binders. Include an index and provide references to the relevant procedures.

Where one procedure interacts with another procedure, make it easy to follow the full process by identifying the reference and the location of the other procedure.

Quick Summary

Key Points
→ You need procedures for consistency, improved results, training and auditing.

→ Involve your staff and users when you develop procedures to ensure accuracy and buy-in.

→ Procedures should be simple and easy to use.

Executive Tips
→ Use modern techniques to develop effective procedures.

→ Focus on the key steps and decision points and give your staff more latitude to use their expertise.

Traps to Avoid
→ Don't develop procedures in isolation.

→ Don't make them long and tedious to use.

Your Action Plan

Based on what you've read, what do you plan to do to improve your ability to influence with your writing?

What are you going to do?	When

Notes

_____

_____

_____

_____

_____

_____

_____

_____

_____

_____

_____

_____

_____

Index

About the Author

Michel Theriault is Principal of *Success Fuel for Managers*, a training & consulting firm providing strategic and management support that helps managers assess, analyze, develop and implement initiatives to get better results.

Other books by the Author

Quick Guides for Managers (Series)
Various Titles

Win More Business - Write Better Proposals
Published March, 2010

Managing Facilities & Real Estate
Published December 2010

Contact Information

Please feel free to connect with me.

Blog: www.successfuelformanagers.com

Twitter: www.twitter.com/micheltheriault

LinkedIn: www.linkedin.com/in/micheltheriault

E-mail: michel@successfuelformanagers.com

www.ingramcontent.com/pod-product-compliance
Lightning Source LLC
Chambersburg PA
CBHW060615210326
41520CB00010B/1346